Preparations for a
Move of God …
In Your Life

BY

Sandra G. Kennedy

All Scripture quotations are taken from the *King James Version* of the Bible. All emphasis within quotations is the author's addition.

Preparations for a Move of God . . .*In Your Life*

ISBN-13: 978-0-7684-1829-3
ISBN-10:   0-7684-1829-1
eISBN-13: 978-0-7684-1828-6

Formerly *Preparations for a Move of God*
(Formerly ISBN 0-9643117-1-2)

Reprinted 2009, 2017

Published by Sandra Kennedy Ministries
2621 Washington Road
Augusta, GA 30904

Table of Contents

❧❧

INTRODUCTION

Often times there are areas in our lives in which we need God to intervene. As we face these challenges, we must put ourselves in a position of faith and expectancy so God has freedom to move on our behalf. To properly prepare for God to move in our lives, we must settle several fundamental truths in our hearts and apply them. If we will do this, our lives will be forever transformed.

We must acquire and live by foundational principles of faith if we are to be overcomers. This is the greatest hour for the Church of Jesus Christ and the time for God's people to truly be a light in the darkness. We must get ready for what God is about to do. We cannot afford to wait until we see the move of God happening before we begin our preparations.

Now is the time to make *Preparations for a Move of God In Your Life.*

Chapter 1

IS JESUS THE SON OF GOD?
If He Is, How Does It Affect Your Life?

৵৵৽

Hebrews 1:1-2a
1 - God, who at sundry times and in divers manners spake in time past unto the fathers by the prophets,
2 - Hath in these last days spoken unto us by his Son ...

There are several questions that we must ask ourselves if we are to be prepared for a move of God. The first issue is this: *Is Jesus the Son of God*? You may say, "How ridiculous! Of course I believe that Jesus is the Son of God. What kind of Christian do you think I am? It's absurd to think that I might believe otherwise". If your reaction to my question is similar to the response given, then you have taken my inquiry much too lightly. This is not just a theological position to which I am referring. It is a fundamental decision that will affect your whole life. It is a serious issue; one which many of us in the Church have not earnestly considered. Many of us have not firmly settled the issue of who Jesus really is to us.

You may be wondering how I could say such a thing. I base my statement on what I have observed in my own life and in the lives of other Christians.

Our lives outside the church building usually do not reflect what we profess with our mouths while we are inside the church building. We still live the same old way that we lived before we made a profession of faith in Jesus. We still do the same old things. We still say the same old words. We still think the same old thoughts. We still go to the same old places. We still spend our money on the same old things. We still watch the same old garbage on television. We still go to the same old rotten movies, or we still rent the same old raunchy videos. The only thing that has changed is where we go Sunday morning. It is obvious that what we profess with our mouths in the church building is not what we believe in our hearts outside the church building. Our daily lives have not been touched.

The question of whether or not Jesus is the Son of God is not an issue of the head; it is an issue of the heart. Many people in churches throughout the world know in their heads that Jesus is the Son of God, and out of this head knowledge they will confess, "Jesus is the Son of God". The words they speak, however, have no power within them. The words have no meaning to them personally. These people are merely parroting what they have heard others say. Although they are confessing the truth, it has about the same impact on their lives as does the reciting of "Peter Piper picked a peck of pickled peppers...." It is just another piece of information stored in their minds. Is our knowledge of Jesus Christ real to us or is it just another historical fact about a man who lived almost two thousand years ago? Does knowing that Jesus is the Son of God have more impact on us than knowing that George Washington was the first President of the United States? Knowing that Jesus is the Son of God must go beyond our heads; it must drop into our hearts. When this happens, we will possess what we know, and our lives will be drastically changed.

When we settle the fact that Jesus is the Son of God, we will realize that He deserves more than one hour of our attention and devotion each week. He deserves more than a recited prayer or confession. He deserves more than the singing of two or three familiar hymns with no thought for what the words that are being sung really mean. He deserves more than our pocket change "guilt offering" that we throw in the offering plate as it passes by us. Jesus deserves to be Lord of **every** aspect of our lives. The real issue is not merely a knowledge of the fact that He is the Son of God, but allowing that truth to infiltrate and change every area of our lives. The real issue is lordship. If Jesus is the Son of God, He should be Lord of every facet of our lives. Change is the indicator of the areas He has touched. If He is Lord over our finances, the change in our spending and giving habits will be evident in our checkbooks. If He is Lord over our families, the change will be evident in the way we treat each other in the privacy of our own homes. If He is Lord over our jobs, the change will be evident in our performance on a daily basis. If He is Lord over our recreational activities, the change will be evident in the activities we choose and the attitude that we have towards them. Every area of our lives should be surrendered to the Lordship of Jesus.

Lordship can be determined by one thing: Who do we obey? If we truly believe that Jesus is the Son of God, we will heed what He has said to us. We will obey His Word. We will not dare to go against what He has commanded. We will not act as if He spoke of impossible things that He never really expected us to do. "Love your enemies" and "turn the other cheek" will not be outdated philosophies, but a way of life (Matthew 5:44, 39). We will no longer commit murder in our hearts by hating someone (Matthew 5:21-22). We will no longer commit adultery in our hearts by thinking lustful thoughts about another person (Matthew 5:27-28). If we really believe that Jesus is the Son of God, we will be givers of our money rather than slaves to it (Luke 6:38; Matthew 5:24). Do we live as if we really believe the words of Jesus?

Knowing and believing that Jesus is Lord will also change how we view our situations and circumstances. If He is Lord, then He is bigger than all of our problems. The key to our victory is the perspective from which we choose to view things. If we focus all of our time and attention on our problems, they will become more real to us than God is. Talking about our problems brings life to them. We are guilty of doing this even when we pray. We need to quit telling God about our big problems and start telling our problems about our big God. When **He** becomes the focus of our attention, everything else will pale in the light of His glory. Jesus is Lord, and we need to start living accordingly.

> 2 Corinthians 13:5
> Examine yourselves, whether ye be in the faith; prove your own selves. Know ye not your own selves, how that Jesus Christ is in you, except ye be reprobates?

Chapter 2

IT TAKES FAITH TO KNOW GOD

ल९७

Hebrews 11:6
But without faith it is impossible to please
him: for he that cometh to God must believe
that he is, and that he is a rewarder of them
that diligently seek him.

Without faith, nobody can believe that Jesus is
the Son of God. This brings us to the second basic
truth which is this: *It takes faith to know God.*
Once again you may be offended at the simplicity
of the statement, but this is another basic issue that
the Church has failed to teach and demonstrate.
The Bible says in Hebrews 11:6 that we must have
faith to know God, to please God, and to receive
from God. He desires for us to seek Him and to
find Him. We act as if He is sometimes hiding
from us, but God wants us to know Him. He is
constantly seeking us even when we do not want to
be found. All of history, from the Garden of Eden
to the present, is God's pursuit of man. God is on a
great "manhunt". He is looking for people who
will believe Him and seek Him with all that is
within them. He promises to reward those who will
come after Him. And the greatest reward is God

Himself. Just to know Him is reward enough to seek Him with all that is within us.

The truth of this verse has absolutely transformed my own life. There has never been a time when I have diligently sought God and not found Him. He has always been faithful to meet me and bless me with His Presence. The seeking has not always been easy, but God has always been faithful to "show up". When I take the time to seek the face of the Lord for a specific reason, it sometimes takes two or three days before I can get my mind to calm down enough for me to hear Him. No matter how difficult it is, I choose to set my face like a flint, and I remind God of His promise: "Lord, You said that if I will diligently seek you, I will find You. Well, Lord I'm diligently seeking You, and I expect to find You. And I'm not leaving until I do find You and hear from You". I keep praying this way until I find Him. I do not give up and go back to business as usual if I do not get an answer during the first ten minutes of prayer. I stay on my face until I have what I am seeking. I stay until I hear from Him. The whole process is one of faith. I choose to believe that God is and that He rewards those who diligently seek Him.

So what is faith? Faith is the substance whereby we get things from the unseen to the seen. It has been said that "faith is the currency of heaven". God has already created everything we need in the spiritual realm. He is just waiting for us to call what we need from the spirit realm into the natural realm. We do this by faith. We are to call those things that be not as though they were, and by faith, they will be.

Faith is "volitional surrender and obedience in spite of the circumstances". In this definition of faith, I see two keys. One, faith is a choice. We can choose to believe God or we can choose not to believe God. Our choice does not affect Him; it affects us. Just because someone chooses not to believe that God exists does not make Him nonexistent (Romans 3:3). The same is true for any other Biblical truth. Some denominations of the Church today do not believe that God still heals people physically. Their unbelief does not change the fact that God is the Healer. He heals broken and sick bodies every day, but probably not in any of their services. The second truth that I see in this definition is that faith is not moved by what is happening. Faith is not preoccupied with situations and circumstances. Faith recognizes and acknowledges the Lordship of Jesus Christ in the midst of the circumstances. Faith is not shaken by what it observes on the outside, but stands firmly on Who it knows on the inside. We can choose to have faith in God in spite of our circumstances.

Faith is the ability to turn stumbling blocks into stepping stones. In order for this to happen we must settle the fact that God is a good God - all of the time. We must know this or we will think God has forgotten us or gone on vacation when we are

17

in the middle of a crisis. We must determine in our hearts before the crisis hits us that He loves us and cares for us. If we believe this, then we can know that God is working on our behalf in the midst of the crisis. That is the time when we must remain calm and confident in the love and grace of God. We cannot afford to act like a "bat out of a high pine" (acting in haste). And this is exactly what we will do if we do not believe that our God is a good God. When situations and circumstances are at their worst, He is working on our behalf so that we will be victorious. God will never allow anything to come our way to destroy us. He always provides a way for us to overcome and be victorious. The very thing that the devil intends to use for our destruction, God will use as a springboard to our victory. That which is intended to cause us to stumble can be the stepping stone to higher ground.

Chapter 3

YOU HAVE A MEASURE OF FAITH
Given to You by God

&ev&

Romans 12:3
For I say, through the grace given unto me,
to every man that is among you, not to think
of himself more highly than he ought to
think; but to think soberly, according as **God
hath dealt to every man the measure of
faith.**

The fact that God requires faith from us leads to
the next issue: *Where do we get faith?* Praise God,
He gives faith to us. He so desires for us to know
Him and to trust Him that He has given to us the
faith to do so. Every person has the ability to
believe that God is God and that Jesus Christ is His
Son. God has given enough faith to us to enable us
to reach out to Him.

Each one of us has been given the "measure of
faith". This measure is the amount that is needed
for the situation at hand. If we need healing, God
has given to us the amount of faith necessary to
believe Him and to receive our healing. If we need
a financial breakthrough, God has given to us the
amount of faith necessary to get the finances
required. If we need deliverance from a habit, God
has given to us the amount of faith necessary

free us from that bondage. No matter what the need is, God has given to us the exact measure of faith that we need to be victorious in that area. We have within us the ability to get through anything that comes our way. We can be victorious!

Since God has given faith to every person, we cannot use the lack of faith as an excuse for our actions and attitudes. The problem is not whether or not we have faith; the issue is what we do with the faith we have. Faith is a principle that works all of the time. We put our faith in the power of electricity every time we turn on a light or an appliance. We put our faith in the law of aero-dynamics every time we get into an airplane. We put our faith in the power of the gasoline engine every time we turn the ignition switch in our cars. We not only trust the objects of our faith to do what they were intended to do, we also trust the people who manufactured those objects. It would be foolish for us to invest our time and our money in a product that is not produced by a reputable manufacturer. When we make a purchase, we are in essence saying that we believe that the manufacturer has produced a quality product that will properly do what it was intended to do. When we examine our lives, we realize that we operate in the arena of faith in almost everything we do.

We all have faith, but all of us do not use that faith in a positive way. The object of our faith determines the power and effectiveness of our faith. When we are sick, do we believe the medical report of the doctor or do we believe the Word of God? If our faith is in the doctor's report, we will die. If our faith is in the Word of God, we will live. If our faith concerning our eternal destiny is in our own righteous efforts, we will end up in hell; however, if our faith is in the blood of Jesus and His righteousness, we will end up in heaven (Ephesians 2:8). In every area of our lives, we need to consider the object of our faith. The Bible says that our "faith should not stand in the wisdom of men, but in the power of God", (1 Corinthians 2:5). If our faith is in God, there will be life, joy, peace, and victory. If our faith is not in God, there will be death, depression, turmoil, and defeat. We have faith, but is it in God or something else?

To have faith in someone requires that we trust them. Trust is a product of integrity. We trust those people who are true to their word. The same is true with God. We can trust Him because He and His Word are one. What the Word says is what God says. The integrity of God's Word produces faith. He cannot tell a lie. Since many people these days do not mean what they say, it is hard for us to believe that God means what He says. We must remember Numbers 23:19: "God is not a man, that he should lie; neither the son of man, that he should repent: hath he said, and shall he not do it? or hath he spoken, and shall he not make it good"? He is a good God, and He will do what He says He will do.

To have faith in God's Word, we must know His Word. The Bible is our "lifetime warranty". It spells out our rights, privileges, and responsibilities as children of God along with His rights, privileges, and responsibilities as our Lord. When we know His Word, we will be able to direct our faith in that direction and walk in the victory that Jesus has provided for us.

God has graciously given to us the measure of faith that we need for the situation at hand. We have the choice of whether or not to put that faith in Him. Will we take Him at His Word and put our faith in the integrity of His Word? Victory is ours if we will only believe Him.

Chapter 4

FAITH GROWS
According To What You Do With It

⚮

2 Thessalonians 1:3
We are bound to thank God always for you, brethren, as it is meet, because that **your faith groweth** exceedingly, and the charity of every one of you all toward each other aboundeth;

We have already discussed the fact that God has given to us the measure of faith, but what we do with that faith is entirely up to us. If we look at faith in the Bible, we realize that there are different levels of faith. There is little faith, great faith, strong faith, weak faith, healing faith, shipwrecked faith, and overcoming faith (Matthew 14:31, 15:28; Romans 4:20, 14:1; Acts14:9; 1 Timothy 1:19; 1 John 5:4). From these verses we see that everyone does not necessarily live on the same level of faith. We can have faith and use it fully, partially, or not at all. Our goal should be to develop our measure of faith to the extent that it is overcoming faith, (1 John 5:4). Our faith will grow according to what we do with it.

Faith, in the spiritual realm, is like muscles in the natural realm. Faith has the potential to increase in size, strength, and endurance just as

23

muscles do. If we eat nutritional foods and exercise our muscles, we will grow stronger. On the other hand, if we eat "junk food" and exert ourselves as little as possible, we will grow weaker. The same is true with faith. Our faith grows just as a muscle grows: by feeding it and exercising it. The Word of God is the "food" of faith, and obedience to that Word is the "exercise" of faith. Just as we each have the potential to have strong, healthy muscles, we each can have strong, healthy faith. The choice is ours to make: firm faith or flabby faith.

Faith Grows By Feeding It

Romans 10:17
So then faith cometh by hearing, and hearing by the word of God.

The first step to build our faith is to hear the Word of God. We should be sure that we stay under the teaching of God's Word through the local church, and we should spend personal time in the Word on a daily basis. Just as our physical bodies need to be fed daily to function properly, so must our spirits be fed daily to function properly. Some of us would literally starve to death if we fed our bodies as often as we feed our spirits. One meal on Sunday morning is not enough on which to live for the remainder of the week because faith comes by hearing and hearing and hearing ….

If we expect to be strong spiritually and live in overcoming faith, we must maintain a steady diet of the Word of God. We need to constantly tell ourselves what God says about Himself, about us, and about our situations. We need to tell ourselves that God is a good God (Psalm 106:1) and that He is on our side (Romans 8:31). We need to tell ourselves that we are "the head and not the tail" (Deuteronomy 28:13). We are "more than conquerors" through Christ Jesus (Romans 8:37). We are new creatures in Christ; old things have passed away and all things are new (2 Corinthians 5:17). As we talk to ourselves this way, we build our faith in the Word of God.

Our faith will be in what we are hearing. If we are constantly talking about the problem, our faith will be in the problem. If we are constantly talking about the Solution, our faith will be in Him. We need to wake up and be smart enough to build our faith in the Solution, not in the problem. Along these same lines, we must realize that we cannot afford to surround ourselves with negative people. Their negative attitudes will begin to shake our faith, and we will eventually find ourselves reasoning between God's Word and their negative word. As soon as we try to reason things out, we are in trouble. We must protect our faith by putting ourselves in the proper environment for faith to grow.

Many of us have been raised in denominations where we were taught things that are contrary to the Word of God. Teachings that we heard in Sunday School and in church actually undermined our faith in God. Healing is an example of this. Many of us have been taught all of our lives that miracles are not for today. Because of these teachings, our faith has not been fortified in the area of healing. The Bible says that God never changes (Malachi 3:6) and that Jesus is the same yesterday, today, and forever (Hebrews 13:8). If He has ever been the Healer, He is still the Healer. In areas such as this where we have little or no faith, we must renew our minds with the truth of the Word of God if we are to have victory in these areas. When we renew our minds, we secure our faith in that particular area. We need to speak the Word to ourselves until we believe what God says more than we believe what man says.

> Romans 12:2
> And be not conformed to this world: but be ye transformed by the renewing of your mind, that ye may prove what is that good, and acceptable, and perfect, will of God.

In any area of our lives where we are not walking in victory, there is a lack of faith. We need to find the Scriptures that specifically deal with the need we have and feed upon those Scriptures until we believe that they are true for us. There are numerous books on the market that have topical listings of Scriptures. Computer software is also available that can do quick searches on specific words and phrases. For those of us who do not have very much time for reading, there are cassette tapes which have Scriptures dealing with certain topics. These are available in word and in song. Investing a few dollars in one or two of these resources can save the time and the effort of trying to find and list the specific Scriptures needed. I believe that God has provided these resources to help us to grow up in faith and to be who He has called us to be.

Faith Grows By Applying It

> James 2:14
> What doth it profit, my brethren, though a man say he hath faith, and have not works? can faith save him?

We must be diligent not only to speak the Word of God, but we must also obey the Word of God. There are many people in the Church who know what to do, but they fail to do it. They know what the Word of God says, and many of them can quote great portions of Scripture, but they have never applied what they know to their lives. The growth of their faith is stunted by their inactivity.

If we go back to our analogy with muscles, we clearly see this truth. Just as proper nutrition is not enough to develop strong muscles, neither is proper spiritual nutrition enough to develop strong faith. At some point, our muscles and our faith have to be put to use. Exercising them will cause them to become stronger and will also build endurance. This involves pushing them to go over and beyond previous expectations. Increasing the resistance (lifting heavier weights) or increasing the repetitions accomplishes this with our muscles. The same is true with faith. When we begin to step out in faith in a certain area, God will allow resistance to come our way. If we are learning to trust God for healing, we can be sure that an opportunity will come our way to put our faith into action. Usually, our first bit of "resistance" will be something relatively minor like a little headache or a sore throat. The next time it may be a headache and a sore throat.

As we get stronger in our faith, we will not only encounter greater resistance (heavier weights), but the frequency and the duration of these encounters may increase (more repetitions). The increase in resistance will build our strength, and the increase in repetitions will increase our endurance. Both are necessary for us to be victorious.

Many of us fail to act on our faith. We are programmed to react in a certain way in almost any given situation, and it is usually not a response of faith. Most of us run for the aspirin when a headache hits us. Our faith is in the aspirin, not in the healing power of the Lord Jesus Christ. If we are truly trying to build faith in that area, then we need to start where we are and pray over that aspirin before we swallow it: "God, please help this aspirin do what it is supposed to do. Help it to get to my head quickly, and let there be no evil side effects. Thank You. In Jesus' Name I pray. Amen". God will honor our sincerity and our honesty. He will meet us where we are and work with the faith that we do have. But He does expect us to grow. He does not want us to depend on the aspirin forever. As we continue to grow in faith, God will put us in a place where we cannot locate an aspirin and require us to exercise our faith at a higher level. As our faith grows, God will bring us into situations where He will be glorified through the exercising of our faith in Him. Every time we apply faith to a situation, He is glorified. As we mature in faith, God will use us to greater degrees for His glory.

Another truth that can be seen in the analogy of muscles is that we can be strong in some areas and weak in other areas. In our physical bodies, this difference can be easily seen. I have the exact same muscles in both of my arms, but because I use my right arm more, it is noticeably stronger than my left arm. The same principle is true with faith. In the areas in which we have fed the Word of God and applied that Word through obedience, we are noticeably stronger. I know people who are "hulks" in the spirit when it comes to believing for healing, but at the same time they are "wimps" when it comes to believing for finances. It all depends upon what we feed ourselves and how much we exercise our faith in a particular area.

True faith will produce action. We need to apply our faith to the situation at hand. We do this by being obedient to God's Word for that particular situation. To act on His Word we must know His Word. When we become one with the Word in our actions, then faith becomes an unconscious reality in our lives – the Word is so real in us, we act out faith.

Chapter 5

FAITH MUST BE OF THE HEART, NOT OF THE HEAD

෭෨

Proverbs 3:5-6
5 - Trust in the LORD with all thine heart;
and lean not unto thine own understanding.
6 - In all thy ways acknowledge him, and he
shall direct thy paths.

As we continue looking at faith, we need to
clarify the meaning of the word "heart". When this
word is used in the Bible, it is not referring to the
physical heart muscle that pumps blood throughout
the body. The biblical "heart" refers to the inner
spirit man (Romans 7:22; 1 Peter 3:4; Romans
10:10). The term "spirit" can be used
interchangeably with the word "heart".

Along these same lines, we need to realize that
man is a tripartite being. I am a spirit, I have a soul
(mind, will, and emotions), and I live in a body. If
the spirit and soul are in unity with each other,
there is victory. The battleground is in the mind. It
is there that we make a choice concerning what we
will believe to be the truth. The information that is
used to make this choice comes through two
channels of knowledge: (1) revelation knowledge
from God, or (2) sense knowledge from our five

senses. We have no other ways to acquire knowledge, so we are building our lives on one or the other. We make a choice to be led by the spirit or by the flesh.

If we desire to be people of faith, we must choose to live from the inside out, being led by the spirit. Our lives must be founded upon revelation knowledge from God, through His Word, if we are to be victorious Christians. Faith is a product of the spirit. We have already seen that the foundation of our faith is the Word of God. Our spirits receive information through the Word while our bodies receive information through the five senses. Our minds receive information from both of these sources and decide which one of the two that we will follow. The problem is that our bodies usually "talk" louder than our spirits do, and our minds respond to the louder one. This is the reason that we are not victorious. Our spirits do not take precedence over all the sense knowledge that has been pumped into us over our entire lifetimes. The key to victory is to get our minds lined up with our spirits. This can only happen if we renew our minds with the Word of God. We need to quit paying attention to what our bodies and unrenewed minds say and start listening to what our spirits say. We must learn to quiet our minds and listen for that "still, small Voice" on the inside.

Our spirits believe the Word no matter what our senses say or our minds think. This means that we can have faith in our hearts and doubt in our heads at the very same moment. For faith to work for us, it must drop from our heads to our hearts. To walk in faith, we must trust our hearts and not our heads.

Mental Assent

As I studied this issue of heart knowledge versus head knowledge, I had to deal with the issue of mental assent. This is one of the most dangerous and deceptive things that I see in the Church. Mental assent recognizes the truthfulness of the Word, but does not act on it. Mental assent sees the truth, admires the truth, and says it is the truth, "but not in my case". Mental assent is agreement in the mind, but not in the heart. It is all talk and no walk.

Mental assent does not require anything from us. It does not require us to act on what we know or to change our lives based on what we know. It gives us an "out" if God does not appear to be doing right. The attitude that many people have concerning healing is a good example of mental assent. These people will agree with the Bible with their heads and with their mouths, but their hearts are far from the truth: "Yes, I know that the Bible says that by the stripes of Jesus we are healed (Isaiah 53:5; 1 Peter 2:24). I know that God sent His Word and healed us (Psalm 107:20). I know all of that healing stuff, **but** it just doesn't work for me". These people give mental assent to the Word, but they have no faith in the Word. When healing is the issue, faith says, "God can and He will". Mental assent says, "God can, **but** I'm not sure that He will". When I am dealing with healing and other issues of faith, people tell me some interesting things: "I know what the Bible says, **but**..." Mental assent always brings a "but" into the picture while faith kicks "buts" out.

When I look at my life and the lives of others in the Church, I realize that many of us think that we are living in faith when we are really operating in mental assent. True faith produces results, and when we are in mental assent, these results are not evident in our lives. The Bible says that God has **already** "blessed us with all spiritual blessings in heavenly places in Christ" (Ephesians 1:3). How many of us are actually living in these blessings? Faith brings possession, and since most of us do not possess the spiritual inheritance that is ours, we must be living in mental assent. Mental assent admires the Word, confesses the Word, but it does not possess the Word.

Mental assent is extremely dangerous and deceptive because the Church acts as if it is genuine faith. We can see the danger and the deception when we consider the fundamental issue of whether or not Jesus is the Son of God. Nobody can come to Jesus and be saved unless the Father draws him to Jesus (John 6:44). How many people have been "saved" as a result of their senses or emotions being stirred by an evangelist rather than their spirits being stirred by God? It is frightening to think that so many people believe that they are eternally secure based on mental assent rather than on true faith in the finished work of Jesus Christ. Just because one has prayed the "sinner's prayer" and confessed that Jesus is Lord does not mean he is saved. The Bible says "That if thou shalt confess with thy mouth the Lord Jesus, **and shalt believe in thine heart** that God hath raised him from the dead, thou shalt be saved" (Romans 10:9). It all goes back to the fact that true faith in Jesus as the Son of God will drastically affect our lives. It is obvious to me that many of us are operating in mental assent in this fundamental area because there have been no changes in our lifestyles. If there is no change, He is not Lord over that part of our lives.

Mental assent also keeps us focused on the past: "I know that God can heal, but I remember that Aunt Susie had the same illness, and we buried her within two weeks after the doctor found her tumor". The Bible says: "**Now** faith is the substance of things hoped for, the evidence of things not seen" (Hebrews 11:1). Faith is in the present; hope is in the future; mental assent is in the past. Hope says, "I'll get it sometime". Faith says, "I've got it now". Mental assent says, "Nobody that I know has ever gotten it before, so I never will either".

Are we walking in faith or mental assent? Do we truly believe that the Bible is the Word of God? If we are disobedient to any commandment, we have mental assent in that area. If we murmur or gossip, we have mental assent. If we think lustful thoughts, we have mental assent. If we have a hateful attitude, we have mental assent. If we walk in unforgiveness, we have mental assent. If we know to do right and we do not do it, we have mental assent. The bottom line is that we act on what we really believe. Do we really believe the Word of God?

Sense Knowledge

Before we move to another principle of faith, I want to look at sense knowledge and revelation knowledge more closely. The first thing we need to understand is the importance of our senses. We tend to take them for granted until one of them is impaired or taken from us in some way. Those of us who wear glasses, contact lenses, or hearing aids can understand this to a certain extent with the senses of seeing and hearing. Our five senses are necessary for meaningful life on earth. Apart from what God has told us, everything that we know has come to us through our five senses; if all five were destroyed, we could not gain any knowledge.

We need to remember that God formed our physical bodies, and He designed them to relate to the physical world through the five senses. He did not, however, intend for us to be ruled and guided by our five senses. His original intent was for man to be ruled from the inside out. Man's spirit, submitted to God's Spirit, was intended to be the one in control of the soul and the body. After the Fall, man was no longer led by the Holy Spirit or by his own spirit, but became dependent upon his senses to lead and guide him. Since then, man has been led and ruled from the outside in.

Jesus met us at our level in the Incarnation. He dealt with us through sense knowledge because we were more tuned to the senses than to the spirit. Jesus came in a body that we could see, hear, and touch. He performed miracles that appealed to all of our senses. He came and showed us how God intended for man to live. Jesus was the first man who chose to be Spirit-led. All of His physical senses were in proper working order, but He chose to hear the Voice on the inside and follow it rather than what His senses told Him. We are to do the same. Jesus made a way for the Holy Spirit to move into us, so we can choose to be Spirit-led people, too.

Our senses connect us with the physical world, and our spirits connect us with the spiritual world. Sense knowledge is based on physical evidence - that which we can see, hear, taste, smell, and feel. Revelation knowledge (spiritual knowledge) is based on spiritual evidence - faith in the Word of God: "Now faith is... the **evidence** of things not seen" (Hebrews 11:1). Sense knowledge is inconsistent, limited, and temporal, while revelation knowledge is consistent, unlimited, and eternal. When we choose to be led by our senses, we become inconsistent, limited in what we can understand and in what we can do, and focused on temporal pursuits that have no real value. Sense knowledge is outside information; revelation knowledge is inside information. Sense knowledge is fact; revelation knowledge is truth. Sense knowledge is based on feelings; revelation knowledge is based on discernment. Sense knowledge will result in defeat; revelation knowledge will result in victory. We are living our lives by the dictates of one or the other.

Abraham is an example of a man who was led by revelation knowledge from God. He chose to turn away from the evidence of his senses and believe what God had said. If Abraham had done as most of us do, then there would have been no Isaac. We would have gone to the mirror and looked at that wrinkled old body everyday. We would have looked across the tent at that little dried up prune of a wife. "Honey, I just don't **see** how we can do this. We are old and well past the years of our fruitfulness, and you were barren even when we were younger. All of the evidence is against us. We should just resign ourselves to the **fact** that we are too old to have children". But Abraham chose to believe God rather than his senses. He chose to believe the truth rather than the facts.

Romans 4:18-21

18 - Who against hope believed in hope, that he might become the father of many nations, according to that which was spoken, So shall thy seed be.

19 - And being not weak in faith, **he considered not his own body** now dead, when he was about an hundred years old, **neither yet the deadness of Sarah's womb**:

20 - He staggered not at the promise of God through unbelief; but was strong in faith, giving glory to God;

21 - And being fully persuaded that, what he had promised, he was able also to perform.

In the New Testament, the disciple Thomas is an example of a man who operated in sense knowledge (John 20:19-29). The first time that Jesus appeared to the disciples in their place of hiding after His resurrection, Thomas was not there. When the disciples told him that Jesus had appeared to them, he did not believe them. Instead of believing their word and the Word of Jesus concerning His death and resurrection, he demanded evidence that he could see and touch: "... Except I shall see in his hands the print of the nails, and put my finger into the print of the nails, and thrust my hand into his side, I will not believe" (John 20:25). Eight days later, Jesus appeared to the disciples again, and Thomas had the evidence standing in front of him. Jesus met Thomas on the sense level, but He rebuked him for his lack of faith: "... Thomas, because thou hast seen me, thou hast believed: blessed are they that have not seen, and yet have believed" (John 20:29).

Most people are led by their five natural senses just as Thomas was. We all have a tendency to demand physical evidence. "I'll believe it when I see it" is the general attitude. Those of us who are Christians are just as guilty of being led by sense knowledge as our unsaved friends and family who are in the world. Churches are full of people who teach or have been taught sense knowledge: "Signs and wonders are not for today. Healing has passed away". The only things that have passed away are those people who did not believe in healing.

We are all products of what we have been taught, and most of us have been taught facts that are based upon sense knowledge. A fact is sense knowledge; a truth is revelation knowledge. Truth supersedes facts. Just as the law of aerodynamics (lift) is a higher law than the law of gravity, so truth is a higher law than fact. A good example of fact versus truth can be seen with healing. I have been involved in conversations of this sort:

"But Pastor, the doctor says that I am going to die".

"The Word of God says that you were healed by the stripes of Jesus. If you were healed, then you are healed".

"I know that, but all of the medical reports say that I have a terminal illness. Nobody has ever been cured".

"Well, God says that He sent His Word and healed you and delivered you from all of your destructions".

"I know that, but my doctor is a specialist in his field, and he knows what he is talking about".

"The truth is that God knows what we need before we even know to ask for it. He knew that you were going to need healing before you even knew you were sick. That's why Jesus bore all of your sickness and disease two thousand years ago".

"I know that, but these are the facts. And facts don't lie. That's just the way it is. The fact is, I am going to die".

"The truth is that you will live and not die and you will declare the glory of the Lord".

"I know that, but..".

This is a classic example of someone who is operating in mental assent based upon information gathered through the senses. With truth staring him in the face, he is not able to get beyond the facts, and he chooses to believe what the doctor says rather than what God says. In this case, the person's faith in the medical report will bring it to pass.

How many of us are living our lives based upon facts rather than truth? I know people who are emotional and spiritual cripples because of what their parents told them when they were children. "You good for nothin' bum. You'll never amount to anything"! After hearing this for years ("Faith comes by hearing"), they internalize what they have heard, and the words become pictures in their minds. The more they see themselves as bums, the more they believe that it is the truth. Today, they are living out what they were told.

We need to be careful what we allow our ears to hear. They are not to be garbage pails. If we cannot avoid those who speak negatively, we must be sure we speak positively to ourselves so that we counteract the negative junk that comes our way. We believe what we say about ourselves more than we believe what others say about us. If we will tell ourselves who God says we are, we will believe what He says rather than the negative things that we hear elsewhere. At the same time, we do not need to allow our mouths to be garbage pails either. We need to be very careful about what we say about others as well as what we say about ourselves. Parents need to especially be aware of the impact of their words on their children. Our words have power: "Death and life are in the power of the tongue..." (Proverbs 18:21). Many of us need to rid ourselves of years of negative sense knowledge. The Word of God is powerful enough to do just that. And the process will not take years if we are diligent to do our part in renewing our minds with the Word.

As we renew our minds, we also build our faith and strengthen our spirits. This process will eventually enable our minds to get beyond all of the sense knowledge and respond to the revelation knowledge. If we do not renew our minds, we will never be in a position where we can be spirit-led people. As Christians, we have a marvelous opportunity to be who God intended us to be. We have a choice. Those who do not know Jesus have nothing to rely upon other than their sense knowledge. Unless they come to Jesus, they will never know anything except what they can see, hear, taste, touch, and smell. They are limited in the ways in which they can deal with things. This is why so many people are depressed and fearful. Those of us who are in the Church appear to be just as depressed and fearful as those who are in the world. We, too, have limited ourselves to the knowledge that we receive from our senses. We must realize that we are not restricted to the realm of the senses. In the spirit realm, there are options that are available to us by faith. There is a whole different way of viewing and living life in the spirit.

We must learn to believe God independently of our senses. We do this by taking our senses to where we are seated - in heavenly places in Christ Jesus (Ephesians 2:6). We must begin to see things from our heavenly perspective and call forth what we see from there. We have to speak it forth from the spirit realm in order for it to be manifested in the natural realm. God has already provided everything we need. He is not limiting us in any way. He is waiting on us to use our faith. We must stop restricting ourselves to sense knowledge and start living in revelation knowledge. We can do all things through Christ. We must let the truth supersede the facts. We need to change our mentality from that of "seeing is believing" to that of "believing is seeing". Will you believe?

Chapter 6

FAITH REQUIRES CORRESPONDING ACTION

જીબ્જી

James 2:14 (J. B. Phillips)
Now what use is it, my brothers, for a man to say he "has faith" if his actions do not correspond with it? Could that sort of faith save any-one's soul?

James 2:17-18, 20, 22, 26
17 - Even so faith, if it hath not works, is dead, being alone.
18 - Yea, a man may say, Thou hast faith, and I have works: show me thy faith without thy works, and I will show thee my faith by my works.
20 - But wilt thou know, O vain man, that faith without works is dead?
22 - Seest thou how faith wrought with his works, and by works was faith made perfect?
26 - For as the body without the spirit is dead, so faith without works is dead also.

The Bible clearly states in James that true faith is always accompanied by corresponding actions. This does not contradict other scriptures concerning faith and works such as Galatians 2:16 and Ephesians 2:8-9. These verses refer to our attempts to make ourselves righteous or worthy. We all know that our efforts to earn God's favor and love are fruitless. The best that we can do is "as filthy rags" in His sight (Isaiah 64:6). The "works" to which James refers are actions that correspond to and back up what we say we believe. These actions say, "I believe what God says about me, and because I believe, I am going to act as if I believe Him".

We discussed in an earlier chapter the fact that faith is required in almost everything we do. To illustrate this truth concerning corresponding actions, let us consider a piece of modern technology of which most of us are aware. A television set is something that many of us have no idea how or why it works. If I were to take a general survey of people and ask them how a television set works, I would probably get replies like this: "Well, I don't really know how it works. All I know is that when I punch that little 'Power' button, a picture shows up on the screen". By faith, not their understanding of electronics, they would tell me that the TV works. If I had a TV with me during the interview, the majority of the people would demonstrate their faith and prove their point by pushing the button to turn on the TV. I might interview someone who would just talk to me about how certain they were that the TV would work. We could both be in agreement that it would work, but neither of us would be convinced until one of us punched that button and turned on the thing. Our faith, our confession, and our agreement would have no value until we actually did something to demonstrate that faith. The same is true for things of the spirit. Our faith and confession in God are of no value to us or to anybody else until we do something to demonstrate our faith. There must be corresponding action.

Most of the time, the corresponding actions of faith will simply be works of obedience. Just living a life of obedience to the will of God is evidence of our faith in Him. It goes back to our fundamental issue: "Is Jesus the Son of God"? If we truly believe that He is, then we will obey His Word.

> Matthew 7:24-27
> 24 - Therefore whosoever heareth these sayings of mine, and doeth them, I will liken him unto a wise man, which built his house upon a rock:
> 25 - And the rain descended, and the floods came, and the winds blew, and beat upon that house; and it fell not: for it was founded upon a rock.
> 26 - And every one that heareth these sayings of mine, and doeth them not, shall be likened unto a foolish man, which built his house upon the sand:
> 27 - And the rain descended, and the floods came, and the winds blew, and beat upon that house; and it fell: and great was the fall of it.

Simon Peter was a professional fisherman. He and his fellow workers had fished all night when Jesus told them to go back out to sea and to throw their nets in the water for a great catch. Peter probably thought Jesus was crazy (refer to Luke 5:1-6). It made no sense to go back out there. They had fished all night with no success, it was the wrong time of the day to fish, and they had just finished cleaning their nets. I imagine Peter's sense knowledge roared to the forefront of his mind, begging him to come to his senses. Thank God, he did not come to his senses. As Peter had been cleaning his nets that day, Jesus had been teaching the Word of God from his boat. Peter could not avoid hearing Him teach, and when Jesus spoke to him personally, faith rose above sense knowledge, and Peter responded to the Word of Jesus: "Master, we have toiled all the night, and have taken nothing: **nevertheless at thy word I will let down the net**" (Luke 5:5). Peter did not just make a confession of faith in the Word of the Lord, but he dropped those nets in the water as an act of obedience. We, too, must reach the point where we will be obedient to God in spite of what our senses tell us. Knowing the will of God is not enough; we must do the will of God.

Another good example of corresponding actions can be seen with healing. If a person receives an evil report from the doctor, his actions will indicate where his faith is. If his faith is in the word of the doctor, he will make plans to die. His corresponding actions will include such things as writing or updating his will, purchasing a cemetery plot, choosing a mortician, picking out songs that he wants to be sung at his funeral, selecting pall bearers, etc. He may confess that Jesus is His Healer, and he may quote every healing scripture in the Bible, but his actions speak louder than his words. He is operating in mental assent, and the sense knowledge received from the doctor and from his body is the object of his faith. If this person's faith is in the Word of God, he will make plans to live. His corresponding actions will include plans for the future such as committing to teach a Sunday School class for the next year, renewing his employment contract, continuing to make contributions into his retirement account, making short and long term goals for spiritual, emotional, physical, and professional growth, making plans for a vacation trip next summer, etc. He will not only confess that Jesus is His Healer and quote healing scriptures, he will also act as if he believes what he is saying is true.

Another example of this principle of corresponding actions is when Peter walked on the water (Matthew 14:22-33). Of the twelve men in the boat, Peter was the only one who had faith for the situation at hand. The other eleven had mental assent and sense knowledge. How can I say that Peter was the only one who had faith? Because he got out of the boat. He had corresponding actions.

From these examples, we see that mental assent and sense knowledge will never act on the Word of God; only faith will act on the Word. Mental assent will admire the Word and confess the Word, but it will never act on the Word. When we really believe God, we will respond to Him. We cannot confess our faith and live contrary to what we say. Our lives cannot contradict our faith. If our actions do not line up with what we say we believe, we are not operating in true faith. We are operating in mental assent and/or sense knowledge. We must do what we confess. We must put our faith into action by living as if we really believe that the Word of God is true. It is not enough to know the Word; we must act on what we know.

When we really believe God for something, we act upon it by making plans to receive it. We will act as if we already have it. In the natural, we prepare for things before we have them. A couple that is planning to have a baby does not wait until the contractions begin before they start preparing the nursery. He that has ears to hear, let him hear....

At this very moment, you are holding in your hands the result of corresponding actions. This book is a result of faith. I believe that we are about to experience the greatest move of God that the Church has ever seen.

Because I believe this, I am making every effort to make preparations for this move of God. I believe this so much that I have written this book to help you to prepare for this move of God. If I did not believe it, I would have done nothing about it.

We will always act on what we really believe. Many times we contradict our confessed "faith" by the way we live. We cannot just talk it; we must also walk it. We must have corresponding actions. Do the people who deal with us on a daily basis know that we believe that Jesus is the Son of God? Do our actions correspond with our words?

Chapter 7

FAITH NEVER RISES ABOVE ITS CONFESSION

∽ುೂ

Mark 11:22-23
22 - And Jesus answering saith unto them, Have faith in God.
23 - For verily I say unto you, That whosoever shall **say** unto this mountain, Be thou removed, and be thou cast into the sea; and shall not doubt in his heart, but shall believe that those things which he **saith** shall come to pass; he shall have whatsoever he **saith**.

Luke 8:11
Now the parable is this: The seed is the word of God.

We have previously mentioned the importance of confessing the Word of God in order to renew our minds and to feed our faith. As we continue to look at this principle of faith, we need to realize that faith never rises above its confession. In other words, we cannot believe one thing and confess another. According to the Bible, "What you say is what you get" is actually a profound truth when faith is mixed with it (Mark 11:23). I am not saying that we will get everything we say, since we make little flippant remarks at times, with no belief that they will ever come to pass. But if we keep making those remarks, we will one day start to believe them. If that happens, what we say will come to pass. We do need to monitor what we say, especially if we say it often. If we do something that is stupid, we should not say, "I'm so stupid"! We are not stupid, but we do occasionally do stupid things. There is a difference between the two. If we must say something, it would be better to say, "That was a stupid thing to do".

Confession can work for us or against us - it all depends upon what we are confessing and believing. The words that we speak are seeds, and we will reap what we sow. If we plant corn in the natural, we do not get a turnip crop. If we want turnips, we must plant turnips. The same is true in the spirit realm. We cannot sow strife and expect to reap peace. If we want peace, we must sow peace. As Christians, the seed that we need to sow is the Word of God (Luke 8:11), but we cannot confess what we do not know. To know the Word, we must spend time listening to and reading the Word. If we are to be victorious, we must know what God says and confess what He says.

Many of us have a mountain that we are facing in our lives. This mountain is the problem that appears to be so big that we cannot get around it, through it, or over it. The Bible says that we are to remove it. The way to do this is to speak faith-filled words to that mountain and to tell it to get out of the way (Mark 11:23). Whatever we say about our problem is what we will get. We must fill ourselves with the Word and believe it in our hearts. We need to find scriptures that specifically address the problem at hand and fire away. It may appear that nothing is happening at first, so we must choose up front to go the way of the Word whether we see anything happening or not. We must keep speaking the Word to that mountain. Every time we speak the Word to that mountain, we are shaking its foundation. We must keep speaking, believing and knowing that we are chipping away a piece at a time. If we will just persevere, we will see that mountain crumble!

God is a faith God who "...calleth those things which be not as though they were" (Romans 4:17). He spoke, and all of creation came into existence at His Word. "And God **said**, Let there be light: and there was light" (Genesis 1:3). He believed what He said, and it came to pass. After creation, God continued to speak. The Bible is full of the promises that God made to us, and He intends for them to come to pass. Everything we need is already in the spirit realm for us because God has already spoken them into being. He is resting in faith, knowing that what He has said will come to pass. He is just watching it happen. All we have to do is what our Father did: call those things that be not as though they were. Now I know what some of you are thinking. "I am not going to tell a lie. You can't make me say something that's not so". My reply to this is, "Well, you do it all the time on the negative end of the spectrum, so why don't you do it on the positive end"? We are constantly calling those things that be not as though they were. Just listen to some of the things we say:

> "You can't go over to that section of town because they will rob you blind".

> "If you drive down that street, you will have a wreck for sure".

> "I always get a sinus infection that time of the year".

> "You know that he comes from bad seed and will never amount to anything".

> "My mama had bursitis. My grandma had bursitis. My uncle's coon dog had bursitis, so I know I'll have it, too".

God help us to turn our confessions around in the other direction. We must start calling positive things in from the spirit realm. We are not lying when we do this. We are simply calling something to us that is in a different location. It is just like calling for a dog to come. When we call for Spot to come, we are calling those things that be not as though they were. We say, "Here, Spot"! And we say this because Spot is not here, and we want him to be here. We call him in from the backyard because we want him to be in the house. After we call him, we wait for him to come. We do not call him and then slam the door shut so he cannot come in the house. It is so simple we can miss it, Church. All that we need - health, money, security, favor, wisdom, peace, joy - is in the "backyard". All we have to do is call it in and wait for it to come! If we do not see it coming immediately, we just need to keep calling until it comes in the house.

As we become more aware of the power of our words, we need to make sure that we confess the truth, not the facts. We have already discussed truth versus facts in a previous chapter, so I will not go into as much detail here. I do want us to look at one instance in the history of Israel where we see the effects of believing and confessing facts versus truth. God had delivered Israel from the hand of Pharaoh through many signs and wonders. From the plagues to the crossing of the Red Sea, God had shown Himself to be the one Who was in control. The place where I want us to pick up the narrative is when the twelve spies were sent into the Promised Land.

Numbers 13:26-14:9
26 - And they went and came to Moses, and to Aaron, and to all the congregation of the children of Israel, unto the wilderness of Paran, to Kadesh; and brought back word

unto them, and unto all the congregation, and showed them the fruit of the land.

27 - And they told him, and said, We came unto the land whither thou sentest us, and surely it floweth with milk and honey; and this is the fruit of it.

28 - Nevertheless the people be strong that dwell in the land, and the cities are walled, and very great: and moreover we saw the children of Anak there.

29 - The Amalekites dwell in the land of the south: and the Hittites, and the Jebusites, and the Amorites, dwell in the mountains: and the Canaanites dwell by the sea, and by the coast of Jordan.

30 - And Caleb stilled the people before Moses, and said, Let us go up at once, and possess it; for we are well able to overcome it.

31 - But the men that went up with him said, We be not able to go up against the people; for they are stronger than we.

32 - And they brought up an evil report of the land which they had searched unto the children of Israel, saying, The land, through which we have gone to search it, is a land that eateth up the inhabitants thereof; and all the people that we saw in it are men of a great stature.

33 - And there we saw the giants, the sons of Anak, which come of the giants: and we were in our own sight as grasshoppers, and so we were in their sight.

Numbers 14

1 - And all the congregation lifted up their voice, and cried; and the people wept that night.

2 - And all the children of Israel murmured against Moses and against Aaron: and the whole congregation said unto them, Would God that we had died in the land of Egypt! or would God we had died in this wilderness!

3 - And wherefore hath the LORD brought us unto this land, to fall by the sword, that our wives and our children should be a prey? Were it not better for us to return into Egypt?

4 - And they said one to another, Let us make a captain, and let us return into Egypt.

5 - Then Moses and Aaron fell on their faces before all the assembly of the congregation of the children of Israel.

6 - And Joshua the son of Nun, and Caleb the son of Jephunneh, which were of them that searched the land, rent their clothes:

7 - And they spake unto all the company of the children of Israel, saying, The land, which we passed through to search it, is an exceeding good land.

8 - If the LORD delight in us, then he will bring us into this land, and give it us; a land which floweth with milk and honey.

9 - Only rebel not ye against the LORD, neither fear ye the people of the land; for they are bread for us: their defence is departed from them, and the LORD is with us: fear them not.

The twelve men who were sent to spy out the land all saw the same things, heard the same things, tasted the same things, and smelled the same things. But when they returned to their own camp, all of them did not confess the same things. Two of them confessed the truth, while ten of them confessed the facts. The two who confessed the truth saw the land through the eyes of faith; the ten who confessed the facts saw the land through the eyes of the flesh. The two who confessed the truth saw the land from God's perspective; the ten who confessed the facts saw the land from their own perspective. The two who confessed the truth compared the giants with their God; the ten who confessed the facts compared the giants with themselves, and as a result, they saw themselves as grasshoppers.

The attitude of the ten spies was detrimental to their faith and to the faith of Israel. It was as if they wanted to spy out the land to see if God had really told them the truth. They found everything to be just as God had told them it would be except for one thing. "God told us the whole truth, but we are here to tell you the facts. God apparently forgot to inform us about the giants in the land. It may be because He did not know they were there. Or if He knew they were there - you know, He may be trying to set us up to destroy us. It would have been better for us to have stayed in Egypt with Pharaoh". They failed to realize that the giants were so insignificant to God that they were not worth mentioning. The giants were not an issue to God so He did not want them to be an issue with Israel. The whole nation was stymied by something that was not even their concern.

As a result of the confession of the ten spies, the whole nation of Israel was led astray by sense knowledge. They chose to believe and confess the facts rather than the truth. Only Joshua, Caleb, Moses, and Aaron saw through the facts and believed and confessed the truth (Numbers 14:5-9). Nobody would listen to them, and that whole generation wandered in the desert until they all died. Only Joshua and Caleb, the two spies who confessed the truth, survived and inhabited the Promised Land.

What are we confessing? Truth or facts? We need to be sure we are observing things through the eyes of faith, not the eyes of the flesh. We need to have God's perspective of the situation - we are seated in heavenly places in Christ Jesus (Ephesians 2:6). We need to compare our big God with our problems rather than comparing ourselves with our big problems. If something is not an issue to God, it should not be an issue with us. If He is not concerned, we should not be concerned. Our confession of faith will remove mountains, bring that which we need from the spirit realm into the natural realm, and determine whether or not we enter into the inheritance that God has prepared for us. What are you confessing?

Revelation 12:11
And they overcame him by the blood of the Lamb, and by the word of their testimony; and they loved not their lives unto the death.

Hebrews 4:14
Seeing then that we have a great high priest, that is passed into the heavens, Jesus the Son of God, let us hold fast our profession.

Proverbs 18:21
Death and life are in the power of the tongue: and they that love it shall eat the fruit thereof.

Chapter 8

BELIEVING IS RECEIVING

❧

Luke 8:11-15
11 - Now the parable is this: The seed is the word of God.
12 - Those by the way side are they that hear; then cometh the devil, and taketh away the word out of their hearts, lest they should believe and be saved.
13 - They on the rock are they, which, when they hear, receive the word with joy; and these have no root, which for a while believe, and in time of temptation fall away.
14 - And that which fell among thorns are they, which, when they have heard, go forth, and are choked with cares and riches and pleasures of this life, and bring no fruit to perfection.
15 - But that on the good ground are they, which in an honest and good heart, having heard the word, keep it, and bring forth fruit with patience.

We have dealt with the fundamental issue of faith: "Is Jesus the Son of God"? We have realized that God has given to us the measure of faith that is required to know Him and to be victorious. We understand that it is our responsibility to feed and exercise our faith so that it can grow. We have seen the dangers of mental assent and sense knowledge, realizing that faith must come from the heart and not from the head. We also know that faith requires corresponding action, and it can never rise above that which we are confessing. Now we need to understand that faith will bring results. If we believe the Word and act on the Word, we will receive the manifestation of the Word. The process through which we go to achieve these results can be seen in the life of Mary, the mother of Jesus, and in the parable of the sower.

The angel Gabriel was sent to Mary to inform her of the thing that the Lord was about to do (Luke 1:26-37). It was at this point that Mary **heard** the Word of the Lord (faith comes by hearing the Word). Next, Mary **believed** the Word and **confessed** her faith in that Word (Luke 1:38, 45). I believe that when she made her confession, "...be it unto me according to thy word", she **conceived** the Word (Luke 1:38). Nine months later, in a donkey stall in Bethlehem, she **received** the manifestation of the Word. I believe that we go through the exact same process today: hear the Word, believe the Word, confess the Word in faith, conceive the Word, and receive the manifestation of the Word.

In the parable of the sower we see that the potential for fruit is inherent in the Word itself, but the seed must fall on fertile soil and be nurtured in order to mature and bring forth fruit (Luke 8:11-15). The soil types in this parable represent the faith levels of different people. The soil "by the way side" represents the person with no faith in the Word (Luke 8:12). The rocky soil represents the person who has mental assent (Luke 8:13). The thorny soil represents the person who has sense knowledge (Luke 8:14). The good soil represents the person who has genuine faith in the Word (Luke 8:15).

God desires to impregnate us with His Word, and He makes a deposit into our lives every time we hear or read the Word. The problem is that it does not always fall on good soil. Many times we have not gone through the necessary steps to prepare our hearts to receive the Word. We need to break up the ground and turn the soil of our hearts so that the seeds will have a place to take root: "For thus saith the LORD to the men of Judah and Jerusalem, **Break up your fallow ground**, and sow not among thorns" (Jeremiah 4:3). At this point we might ask, "How do we do this"? The Bible says, "...Judah shall plow..." (Hosea 10:11), and Judah means "praise". The best thing to do in preparation for the Word is to praise and worship the Lord. There is nothing that will touch and change our hearts as much as rejoicing in our God and basking in His Presence. The soil of our hearts must be ready to receive the Word so that we are able to believe and to conceive the Word.

When seeds are sown in the natural, there is a period of time when nothing appears to be happening. Anyone who has ever planted a seed knows that there is almost always a temptation to doubt that anything is happening to our seed. The best thing to do during this time is to tell others what has been planted. "In this row I have butter beans and sweet potatoes. In those two rows I have corn. In that corner over there, I have watermelons and cantaloupe". Even though the gardener does not yet have any turnips, he still says, "I have turnips here in this row". We should have the same faith and confess that we have what the Word says even though it is not yet evident. "In this area of my life, I have love and kindness. In that part of my life, I have peace. Over in that corner, I have a healthy body". As we do this we are watering those seeds and providing an environment in which they can grow. During this time, faith must be patient and continue to water the seed. We do this by continuing to confess the Word.

Mary continued to confess the graciousness of the Lord when she went to visit with Elizabeth (Luke 1:46-55). She carried the Word of God within her for nine months, doing everything possible to be sure that He would come to full maturity. Only a mother can truly understand the care that is taken to make sure that the precious life within has the best that she can offer. During the incubation period, she monitors everything from the food she eats to the amount of rest she receives. She will even sacrifice things that she enjoys to protect the life of the one she carries. Are we this careful to protect the Word that God has deposited within us? Are we willing to give up some of the things we enjoy to be sure that the development of the Word is not hindered in our lives? I am afraid that many of us abort the Word and never bring forth that which God has deposited within us.

Another truth seen in the parable of the sower and in the example of conceiving a child is that fruit is not always the result of a deposit being made. Every seed that the sower sowed did not bring forth fruit. Every time a deposit of a man's seed is made within a woman, a baby is not conceived. The same is true with the Word of God. Every truth that is deposited within our hearts does not result in the manifestation of that Word. Faith in our hearts produces the atmosphere that is conducive to conception. In order for us to conceive, we must believe.

Last, Mary did not have to beg and plead for Jesus to mature and come forth. The gardener does not have to beg and plead for his crop to come forth. Why, then, do we think that we have to beg and plead with God for His Word to be manifested in our lives? We do not have to beg for those things that are already ours. God says that we have health and prosperity available to us in every area of our lives spirit, soul, and body (3 John 2). The Word may be in seed form now, but it will produce fruit if we will do our part. Will you hear the Word, believe the Word, conceive the Word, and receive the manifestation of the Word in your life?

Luke 1:38
And Mary said, Behold the handmaid of the Lord; be it unto me according to thy word. And the angel departed from her.

Luke 1:45
And blessed is she that believed: for there shall be a performance of those things which were told her from the Lord.

Hebrews 4:14
Seeing then that we have a great high priest, that is passed into the heavens, Jesus the Son of God, **let us hold fast our profession.**

Chapter 9

FAITH: THE WAY OF LIFE

❧

In these closing pages, I would like to encourage you concerning your faith. My prayer is that you will take the things discussed in this book and honestly apply them to your life. As we have progressed through the principles of faith, I trust that one truth, although not directly stated, has penetrated your heart: Faith is a way of life. It is a life of obedience to the Word of God.

Faith will bring about the purposes of God in your life. God knows the call on your life, and He will allow things to come your way to promote you to higher ground. He will test your faith. His intent is that you move up. God wants you to come higher; the higher you go in faith, the more you can see from your heavenly position. Your faith is the key to success. There is no other way to spiritual maturity.

- Faith will always demand that you let go of things that you can see.
- Faith will always bring you into precarious situations…and will always get you out.

- Faith will never fail to cut the ties of your natural safety and dry the springs of your human resources.

Do not be afraid of the situation that looks overwhelming; God is with you. Keep speaking the truth of His Word; talk to yourself until it drops down inside you. Do not let anything move you (situations, circumstances, storms, etc.). Do everything in your power to do what you know is right. Do what you know to do.

Ephesians 6:10-13
10 - Finally, my brethren, be strong in the Lord, and in the power of his might.
11 - Put on the whole armour of God, that ye may be able to stand against the wiles of the devil.
12 - For we wrestle not against flesh and blood, but against principalities, against powers, against the rulers of the darkness of this world, against spiritual wickedness in high places.
13 - Wherefore take unto you the whole armour of God, that ye may be able to withstand in the evil day, and having done all, to stand.

Joshua 1:7-8
7 - Only be thou strong and very courageous, that thou mayest observe to do according to all the law, which Moses my servant commanded thee: turn not from it to

the right hand or to the left, that thou mayest prosper whithersoever thou goest.

8 - This book of the law shall not depart out of thy mouth; but thou shalt meditate therein day and night, that thou mayest observe to do according to all that is written therein: for then thou shalt make thy way prosperous, and then thou shalt have good success.

Deuteronomy 30:11-14, 19

11 - For this commandment which I command thee this day, it is not hidden from thee, neither is it far off.

12 - It is not in heaven, that thou shouldest say, Who shall go up for us to heaven, and bring it unto us, that we may hear it, and do it?

13 - Neither is it beyond the sea, that thou shouldest say, Who shall go over the sea for us, and bring it unto us, that we may hear it, and do it?

14 - But the word is very nigh unto thee, in thy mouth, and in thy heart, that thou mayest do it.

19 - I call heaven and earth to record this day against you, that I have set before you life and death, blessing and cursing: therefore choose life, that both thou and thy seed may live:

Hear the Word. Believe the Word. Speak the Word. Obey the Word. And having done all, STAND!

OTHER BOOKS
DR. SANDRA G. KENNEDY

- ➢ The Simplicity of Healing

- ➢ Proving God

- ➢ The Magnificent Word of The Lord

- ➢ Your Robe of Righteousness

- ➢ The Spirit of Elijah Is In The Land

- ➢ Confessions for Whole Life

- ➢ Prayer Partners' Handbook

For a complete listing of books
and audio teachings
by Dr. Kennedy
call (706) 737-4530
or visit our website at
www.sandrakennedy.org

CONTACT INFORMATION

Sandra Kennedy MINISTRIES
and
Whole Life MINISTRIES

2621 Washington Road
Augusta, Georgia 30904
(706) 737-4530
prayer line (706) 737-2900
e-mail: contact@sandrakennedy.org

websites
www.sandrakennedy.org
www.wholelife.org

The Healing Center
(706) 737-6687
Whole Life Christian Bookstore
(706) 736-3322

to receive the
Sandra Kennedy Ministries E-Newsletter
sign up at our website
www.sandrakennedy.org